WEIRD THINGS
YOU CAN GROW

BY JANET GOLDENBERG
ILLUSTRATED BY PHOEBE GLOECKNER

RANDOM HOUSE 🏠 NEW YORK

Special thanks to

Ed Adams

Jane Clarke

Fina Gloeckner Kalousek

The Kornfield family, especially Esta

Ralph N. Mistler

Barbara Pitschel, Head Librarian,
Helen Crocker Russell Library of Horticulture, San Francisco

Paola Muggia Stuff, Curator, Cartoon Art Museum, San Francisco

Lucy Tolmach, Garden Superintendent,
Filoli Gardens, Woodside, California

Laurence Yep

Ellen Zagory, Nursery Manager,
Davis Arboretum, University of California at Davis

for their help and advice

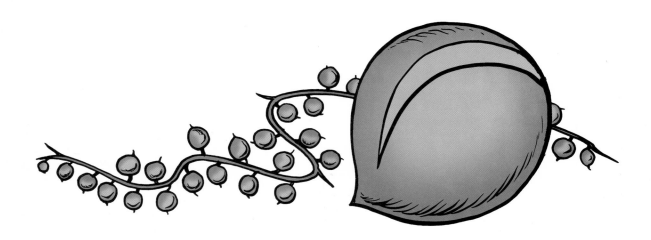

Library of Congress Cataloging-in-Publication Data
Goldenberg, Janet. Weird things you can grow / by Janet Goldenberg ; illustrated by Phoebe Gloeckner.
p. cm. ISBN 0-679-85298-0 1. Gardening—Juvenile literature. 2. Plants, Useful—Juvenile literature.
[1. Gardening. 2. Plants, Useful.] I. Gloeckner, Phoebe, ill. II. Title. SB457.G58 1994 635—dc20 93-43146

Manufactured in the United States of America 10 9 8 7 6 5 4 3 2 1

CONTENTS

INTRODUCTION
Your Weird Garden

A PLANT THAT MOVES WHEN YOU TOUCH IT?!

A CABBAGE YOU CAN USE AS A WALKING STICK?!

AN EGGPLANT WITH REAL-LOOKING "EGGS"?!

STRANGE AND AMAZING THOUGH THEY SEEM, PLANTS LIKE THESE ARE REAL—AND YOU CAN GROW THEM EASILY!!

CAN I SEE?

WEIRD! A COMIC BOOK!

THIS BOOK DESCRIBES 33 BIZARRE PLANTS YOU CAN GROW, INCLUDING WHERE TO GET THEM, HOW TO GROW THEM, AND ODD THINGS ABOUT THEM.

YOU DON'T NEED GARDENING EXPERIENCE TO GROW THESE PLANTS. IN FACT, YOU DON'T EVEN NEED A GARDEN, SINCE MANY OF THEM GROW WELL INDOORS.

THESE ARE JUST A FEW OF THE FASCINATING PLANTS THAT GROW IN THE WORLD—NOT ONLY IN GARDENS BUT IN SWAMPS, DESERTS, MOUNTAINS, RAIN FORESTS, GRASSLANDS, AND EMPTY LOTS.

WE HOPE YOU HAVE FUN LEARNING ABOUT THEM!
—Janet + Phoebe

BUYING WEIRD PLANTS + SEEDS

YOU CAN BUY MANY OF THE PLANTS AND SEEDS IN THIS BOOK AT GARDEN STORES, BUT OTHERS ARE SO WEIRD THAT YOU MAY HAVE TO ORDER THEM BY MAIL. DON'T WORRY! IT'S EASY—MAYBE EASIER THAN SHOPPING IN PERSON!!

YOUR PLANTS ARE HERE!

THAT WAS QUICK!

FRAGILE

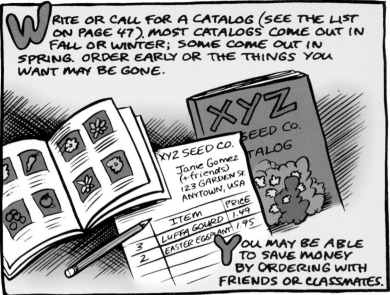

WRITE OR CALL FOR A CATALOG (SEE THE LIST ON PAGE 47). MOST CATALOGS COME OUT IN FALL OR WINTER; SOME COME OUT IN SPRING. ORDER EARLY OR THE THINGS YOU WANT MAY BE GONE.

XYZ SEED CO.
Janie Gomez
(+friends)
123 GARDEN St.
ANYTOWN, USA

	ITEM	PRICE
3	LUFFA GOURD	1.49
2	EASTER EGGPLANT	1.95

YOU MAY BE ABLE TO SAVE MONEY BY ORDERING WITH FRIENDS OR CLASSMATES.

WHEN PLANTS ARRIVE, WATER THEM AND PUT THEM IN A BRIGHT PLACE OUT OF WIND AND DIRECT SUN SO THEY CAN RECOVER FROM THEIR TRIP. (IF THEY ARE INDOOR PLANTS OR IF IT IS WINTER, THIS SHOULD BE INDOORS.)

AFTER A WEEK OR TWO (OR WHEN THE WEATHER WARMS), YOU CAN MOVE THEM TO WHERE THEY WILL GROW.

IF YOU ORDERED SEEDS, KEEP THEM COOL AND DRY UNTIL READY TO PLANT.

WEIRD SEEDS

About Plant Names

GARDEN CATALOGS LIST MANY PLANTS BY THEIR BOTANICAL NAMES (SUCH AS *MIMOSA PUDICA*), RATHER THAN BY THEIR COMMON NAMES (SUCH AS "SENSITIVE PLANT"). THEY DO THIS BECAUSE COMMON NAMES CAN BE CONFUSING: THEY CAN VARY FROM PLACE TO PLACE OR REFER TO MORE THAN ONE PLANT.

TO THE WAY THE PLANT FOLDS UP WHEN TOUCHED. OTHER NAMES HONOR A PERSON OR PLACE. FOR EXAMPLE, THE INSECT-EATING CAPE SUNDEW, *DROSERA CAPENSIS*, IS NAMED FOR THE CAPE OF GOOD HOPE IN SOUTH AFRICA, WHERE IT WAS FIRST FOUND.

THE BOTANICAL NAMES IN CATALOGS HAVE 2 (OR SOMETIMES 3) PARTS: GENUS, SPECIES, AND (SOMETIMES) VARIETY. THEY ARE LIKE A PERSON'S LAST NAME, FIRST NAME, AND NICKNAME.

SEND ME SOME ACTION PLANTS, PLEASE.

SORRY, DEAR. WE ONLY HAVE SENSITIVE PLANTS.

THEY DON'T KNOW IT, BUT THEY'RE BOTH TALKING ABOUT THE SAME PLANT—*MIMOSA PUDICA*.

MANY BOTANICAL NAMES COME FROM LATIN OR GREEK WORDS DESCRIBING THE PLANT; FOR EXAMPLE, *PUDICA*—LATIN FOR "BASHFUL"—REFERS

LAST	FIRST	NICKNAME	
GOMEZ	JANIE	'CURLY'	Curly-haired girl in the Gomez family
GENUS	SPECIES	VARIETY	
ZINNIA	ELEGANS	'ENVY'	Green variety of zinnia

JUST AS PEOPLE RESEMBLE THEIR RELATIVES, PLANTS FROM THE SAME GENUS OFTEN LOOK SIMILAR.

TOOLS AND SUPPLIES

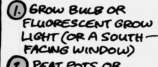

You don't need all the things on this page to grow the plants in this book, but having most of it will help. You'll find them at garden or hardware stores, or maybe even around the house.

INDOOR SEED STARTING

Peat pellets are handy disks of compressed growing medium that expand when soaked.

BEFORE   AFTER

POTTING SOIL

HORTICULTURAL SAND

1. Grow bulb or fluorescent grow light (or a south-facing window)
2. Peat pots or pellets,* or sectioned starting trays
3. Clear plastic bags or plastic take-out salad containers
4. Labels and marker
5. Sterilized potting soil and horticultural sand (not beach sand— it's too salty)
6. Spray bottle and watering can

INDOOR GARDENING

FERTILIZER   IZER

POTTING MIX

CACTUS MIX

HORTICULTURAL SAND

1. Table knife and teaspoon for digging
2. Hand trowel or can for scooping
3. Scissors to snip off dead leaves
4. Containers with saucers (various sizes)
5. Screening, pebbles, or broken pottery to cover drain holes
6. Liquid-feed fertilizer
7. Watering can
8. Potting soils and sand

OUTDOOR GARDENING

COMPOSTER

FERTILIZER PELLETS

HUMUS

1. Spading fork, spade, rake, hoe
2. Hose and sprayer
3. Fertilizer granules or pellets
4. Trellis or fence for vines
5. Homemade compost (rotted leaves and vegetable scraps) or store-bought humus (decomposed organic matter)

GETTING STARTED

ALTHOUGH YOU CAN SOW MANY SEEDS DIRECTLY INTO THE GROUND, MOST WILL START BETTER—AND EARLIER—INDOORS, WHERE YOU CAN CONTROL THE ENVIRONMENT. ONCE THE SEEDLINGS HAVE FOUR LEAVES, YOU CAN TRANSPLANT THEM INTO BIGGER POTS OR MOVE THEM OUTSIDE WHEN FROST HAS ENDED.

SPROUTING SEEDS

SEEDS SPROUT IN SEVERAL DAYS OR WEEKS, DEPENDING ON THE KIND. HERE ARE GENERAL INSTRUCTIONS:

1. PRESS SEEDS INTO MOIST POTTING SOIL AT THE DEPTH NOTED ON THE PACKAGE. LABEL AND COVER WITH PLASTIC.

2. KEEP WARM (70°-80°F) AND BRIGHT. A GROW LIGHT IS IDEAL. (SOME SEEDS LIKE IT COOLER OR DARKER. THE SEED PACK WILL TELL YOU.)

3. AFTER SPROUTING, UNCOVER SEEDLINGS. POUR WATER INTO THE TRAY (NOT THE SOIL) TO AVOID KNOCKING THEM OVER.

TRANSPLANTING INDOORS

YOU CAN ALSO USE THIS METHOD WHEN BIGGER PLANTS OUTGROW THEIR POTS. THE NEW POT SHOULD BE JUST A LITTLE LARGER THAN THE OLD ONE.

POTTING SOIL →

1. COVER THE NEW POT'S DRAIN HOLE WITH SCREENING, PEBBLES, OR BROKEN POTTERY (TO KEEP SOIL IN), AND FILL IT ABOUT HALFWAY WITH POTTING SOIL.

2. USING A TABLE KNIFE, CAREFULLY SLIDE THE PLANT FROM ITS CONTAINER. TRY NOT TO DISTURB THE ROOTS. (SKIP THIS STEP IF USING PEAT POTS OR PELLETS.)

½"

THE BASE OF THE STEM SHOULD BE EVEN WITH THE SOIL

3. SET THE PLANT'S SOIL BALL (OR ENTIRE PEAT POT OR PELLET) INTO THE NEW POT. FILL IN SOIL AROUND IT—SOIL SHOULD BE ½ INCH FROM THE TOP. WATER, THEN ADD EXTRA SOIL IF NECESSARY.

TRANSPLANTING OUTDOORS

MOST PLANTS GROW BEST IN A SUNNY PLACE THAT IS NOT TOO WINDY.

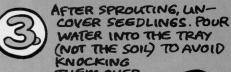

HUMUS

1. AFTER SPRING FROSTS END, BREAK UP SOIL AND RAKE OUT WEEDS AND STONES. MIX IN COMPOST OR HUMUS (ALSO FERTILIZER IF YOU WISH—SEE PAGE 8) AND SOAK WELL.

2. PUT SEEDLINGS OUTSIDE IN A SHELTERED PLACE FOR 1-2 WEEKS, TO GET THEM USED TO THE OUTDOORS. KEEP THEM WATERED!!

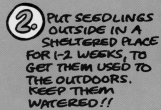

3. IN MOIST SOIL, DIG HOLES AT THE PROPER DISTANCE FROM EACH OTHER (SEE SEED PACK). EASE PLANTS FROM POTS AND PLACE THE BASES OF THEIR STEMS LEVEL WITH THE SOIL LINE. (PEAT CONTAINERS CAN GO RIGHT IN THE GROUND, SINCE ROOTS WILL GROW THROUGH THEM!)

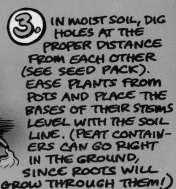

SCATTER FERTILIZER AROUND PLANTS AND WATER THOROUGHLY.

GARDENING TIPS

☼ LIGHT ☼

PLANTS THAT GET TOO LITTLE LIGHT BECOME PALE AND SKINNY, GROW SLOWLY, AND MAY REFUSE TO FLOWER. SYMBOLS IN THIS BOOK TELL YOU HOW MUCH LIGHT EACH PLANT NEEDS.

FULL SUN
AT LEAST 4-5 HOURS OF DIRECT SUN A DAY, PREFERABLY OUTDOORS.

SOME SUN
AT LEAST 1-3 HOURS OF SUN OUTDOORS, OR BY A SOUTH OR WEST WINDOW.

BRIGHT SHADE
INDIRECT SUN, SUCH AS BY A NONSUNNY WINDOW OR UNDER A THIN TREE.

○○ WATER ○○

THE AMOUNT OF WATER A PLANT NEEDS DEPENDS ON WHERE IT CAME FROM. DESERT PLANTS NEED VERY LITTLE; SWAMP PLANTS NEED A LOT. EXCEPT FOR WATER PLANTS, IT'S BETTER TO WATER TOO LITTLE THAN TOO MUCH, SINCE CONSTANT WETNESS CAN SUFFOCATE THE ROOTS.

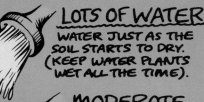

LOTS OF WATER
WATER JUST AS THE SOIL STARTS TO DRY. (KEEP WATER PLANTS WET ALL THE TIME).

MODERATE WATER
LET THE TOP OF THE SOIL DRY OUT BETWEEN WATERINGS.

SOME WATER
LET THE SOIL DRY THOROUGHLY BEFORE WATERING.

🟤 FERTILIZER ✏

IF YOUR SOIL CONTAINS LOTS OF COMPOST OR HUMUS, YOU MAY NOT NEED FERTILIZER. BUT ADDING SOME WILL HELP MOST PLANTS GROW BETTER BY SUPPLYING EXTRA NITROGEN, PHOSPHORUS, AND POTASSIUM.

LIQUID-FEED TYPES
ARE BEST SUITED FOR POTTED PLANTS. YOU ADD A SMALL AMOUNT TO THE WATER.

GRANULE OR PELLET TYPES
ARE BEST SUITED FOR GARDEN PLANTS. YOU WORK IT INTO THE SOIL BEFORE PLANTING, OR SCATTER IT AROUND PLANTS AND WATER IT IN.

THERE ARE MANY DIFFERENT FORMULAS, WITH DIFFERENT PERCENTAGES OF THE THREE NUTRIENTS. HIGH-NITROGEN FORMULAS (SUCH AS 20-6-12) ARE BEST FOR LEAFY PLANTS. HIGH-PHOSPHORUS FORMULAS (SUCH AS 5-10-5) ARE BEST FOR FLOWERS AND FRUIT.

PESTS + DISEASES

PLANTS IN GOOD SOIL WITH ENOUGH LIGHT, WATER, AND FERTILIZER TEND TO STAY HEALTHY. YOU CAN PREVENT MANY PROBLEMS BY TAKING GOOD CARE OF YOUR GARDEN.

REMOVE WEEDS AND DEAD LEAVES, WHERE PESTS CAN HIDE.

IF PESTS EAT YOUR PLANTS, PICK THEM OFF BY HAND, BLAST THEM WITH A HOSE, OR SPRAY THEM WITH A MIXTURE OF WATER AND LIQUID SOAP.

CUTWORM

YOU CAN FENCE OUT CUTWORMS WITH CARDBOARD MILK CARTONS.

SOME PESTS (SUCH AS SNAILS) YOU CAN TRAP AND CRUSH.

(1.) LOOKS NICE AND SHADY IN HERE! ? · NEW

(2.)

(3.) CRUNCH

HELP PREVENT LEAF DISEASES BY KEEPING THE LEAVES DRY WHEN YOU WATER.

WATER IN THE MORNING SO LEAVES CAN DRY BY DARK.

CUT OFF MILDEWED OR PUCKERED LEAVES AND THROW THEM IN THE TRASH— THEY HAVE A PLANT DISEASE. IF THE PLANT STAYS SICK, YOU MAY HAVE TO DISCARD IT.

TRASH

SNIP!

CHAPTER 1
Weird and AMAZING

All plants are weird in some way, but some are much weirder than others. The plants in this chapter are truly incredible — and remarkably easy to grow!!

HOW THEY GOT THAT WAY
According to the theory of evolution, all plant traits — weird or not — arise by accident.

Some endure because they help the plant solve a problem in its environment.

PROBLEM: Too dark on forest floor.

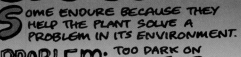

SOLUTION: Perch on trees.

BUTTERFLY ORCHID (EPIDENDRUM TAMPENSE)

PROBLEM: Hot sun burns leaves.

SOLUTION: Cover them with fuzz.

PANDA PLANT (KALANCHOE TOMENTOSA)

Other traits survive by chance or because plant breeders like them.

WILL YA LOOK AT THIS TULIP THAT CAME UP?

WE COULD SELL A MILLION OF 'EM!!

PARROT TULIP

PLANTS
From similar environments often evolve similar traits, even though they aren't related. Biologists call this "convergent evolution."

In the ocean, many seaweeds have air pockets that help them float.

FUCUS FURCATUS   MACROCYSTIS INTEGRIFOLIA

MAPLE (ACER SPECIES)   ELM (ULMUS SPECIES)

In cold climates, many trees shed their leaves for winter. Strangely enough, this helps to keep them from freezing.

In the desert, many plants have thick leaves or stems that store water.

PENCIL PLANT (EUPHORBIA TIRUCALLI)   LACE CACTUS (MAMMILLARIA ELONGATA)

SENSITIVE PLANT

(MIMOSA PUDICA)

MOST PLANTS MOVE SLOWLY, USUALLY TOWARD THE SUN. BUT THE SENSITIVE PLANT—A BRAZILIAN MEMBER OF THE PEA FAMILY—CAN MOVE EXTREMELY FAST. WHEN YOU TOUCH ITS LEAFLETS OR DRIP WATER ON THEM, THEY SUDDENLY FOLD TOGETHER AND THE LEAF STEM DROPS DOWN!

IF YOU HIT A LEAF EVEN HARDER, MANY STEMS WILL DROP, EVEN THOUGH THEY WEREN'T ALL TOUCHED.

WHY? NO ONE KNOWS EXACTLY. SOME BOTANISTS THINK IT IS TO PROTECT THE LEAVES FROM TOO MUCH WIND, WHICH CAN DRY THEM OUT.

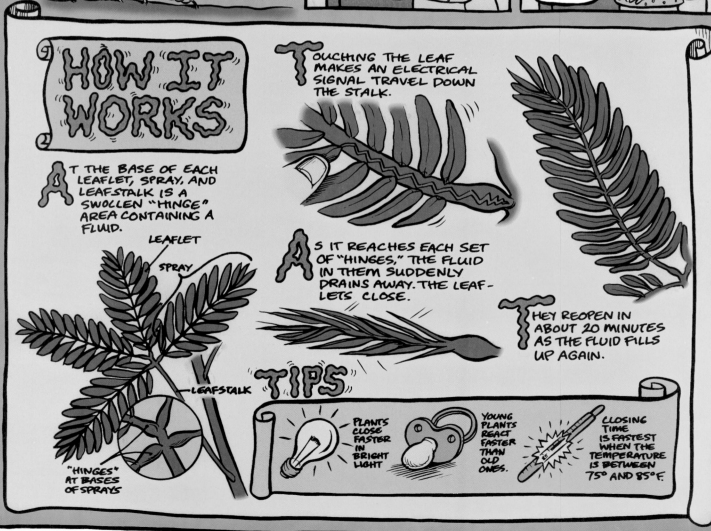

HOW TO GROW

FULL SUN

INDOORS/OUTDOORS/

MODERATE WATER

GET SEEDS BY MAIL* (SOME STORES MAY HAVE THEM.) SOAK THEM IN HOT TAP WATER FOR 20 MINUTES.

* SEE "WHERE TO GET THEM" ON PAGE 47.

PLACE SEEDS ON TOP OF MOIST POTTING SOIL. SEAL IN PLASTIC UNDER A GROW LIGHT OR BY A BRIGHT (NOT SUNNY) WINDOW.

TRUE LEAVES APPEAR AND BECOME SENSITIVE ABOUT A WEEK AFTER SEEDS SPROUT.

TRUE LEAF

SEED LEAF

YOU CAN MOVE PLANTS TO BIGGER POTS (OR OUTSIDE IN THE SUMMER).

SEE? I'M TRANSPLANTING IT!!

IF LEAVES START TO TURN YELLOW, USE LIQUID FERTILIZER ONCE A WEEK.

+ (M T W TH F S SU) =

THE AMAZING TELEGRAPH PLANT
(DESMODIUM MOTORIUM)

SENSITIVE PLANTS MOVE WHEN TOUCHED, BUT THIS INCREDIBLE PLANT MOVES ALL BY ITSELF! ON WARM, SUNNY DAYS, TWO SIDE LEAFLETS OF EACH LEAF MAKE SLOW CIRCLES IN THE AIR. *NO ONE KNOWS WHY!!!*

ALSO A MEMBER OF THE PEA FAMILY, THIS PLANT FROM THE ASIAN TROPICS CAN BE GROWN OUTSIDE IN WARM CLIMATES.

UNFORTUNATELY, SEEDS ARE HARD TO GET!!

WHOA! I'M GETTING DIZZY!

MOVING LEAFLETS

NICE BREEZE HERE!

VENUS FLYTRAP

(DIONAEA MUSCIPULA) AND OTHER CARNIVORES*

THIS NOTORIOUS PLANT HAS A NASTY LITTLE HABIT: WHEN A BUG LANDS ON ITS JAWLIKE LEAVES, THEY CLAMP SHUT AND DIGEST IT. WHY? INSECTS SUPPLY HARD-TO-GET NUTRIENTS IN THE BOGGY PLACES WHERE THIS PLANT GROWS.

VENUS FLYTRAPS GROW WILD IN ONLY ONE REGION ON EARTH: NORTH AND SOUTH CAROLINA. BECAUSE THEIR WETLAND HABITATS ARE DISAPPEARING, THESE AMAZING PLANTS ARE BECOMING RARE.

1. A BUG LANDS ON THE TRAP, JIGGLING ONE OF ITS TRIGGER HAIRS TWICE— OR TWO HAIRS ONCE. IF THERE'S JUST ONE JIGGLE, THE TRAPS STAYS OPEN.

2. SENSORY CELLS NEAR THE JIGGLED HAIR(S) SEND AN ELECTRICAL SIGNAL TO NEARBY MOTOR CELLS. THESE EMPTY OF FLUID AND COLLAPSE, SPRINGING THE TRAP SHUT.

3. THE TRAP STAYS PARTWAY OPEN SO SMALLER BUGS CAN ESCAPE (THEY'RE NOT WORTH THE EFFORT OF DIGESTING). SPECIAL GLANDS TASTE THE PREY. IF IT'S NOT EDIBLE, THE TRAP REOPENS IN ABOUT 12 HOURS.

4. THE BUG'S MOVEMENT STARTS THE TRAP'S DIGESTIVE JUICES FLOWING AS THE TRAP SQUEEZES SHUT.

5. 1-3 WEEKS LATER... DIGESTION COMPLETED, THE TRAP OPENS AND THE BUG'S DRIED-UP REMAINS BLOW AWAY. A TRAP CAN CATCH UP TO 3 BUGS BEFORE WITHERING.

CLAMP!

HELP ME!

HMM?

TRIGGER HAIR

* MEAT EATERS

HOW TO GROW

FULL SUN

INDOORS/OUTDOORS (SUMMER OR WARM CLIMATES)

LOTS OF WATER

BUY ONLY A NURSERY-GROWN PLANT... IF IT CAME FROM THE WILD OR IF YOU'RE NOT SURE, DON'T BUY IT.

FEROCIOUS CARNIVOROUS PLANTS

YOU DIDN'T GET THESE PLANTS FROM THE BOG, DID YOU, MISTER?

OH, NO! WE GREW THIS HERE *DIONAEA MUSCIPULA* JUST FOR YOU!

GOOD! Y'ALL KNOW THEY'RE ENDANGERED!

KEEP YOUR FLYTRAP STANDING IN DISTILLED OR FILTERED WATER, OR RAINWATER. (MOST TAP WATER CONTAINS MINERALS THAT CAN KILL IT). <u>NEVER</u> ADD FERTILIZER.

IN WINTER, KEEP YOUR PLANT DRYISH AND COOL (40°–50° F). THE LEAVES WILL DIE BACK, BUT MORE WILL GROW IN SPRING.

DISTILL WATER

IN SUMMER, LEAVE YOUR FLYTRAP OUTDOORS SO IT CAN CATCH BUGS. IT CAN SURVIVE WITHOUT CATCHING ANYTHING. BUT YOU CAN FEED IT A LIVE FLY OR A SMALL SLUG NOW AND THEN. (HAMBURGER OR OTHER "HUMAN" FOOD MAY ROT THE TRAPS).

UH-OH!

MORE CARNIVORES

HERE ARE TWO OTHER EASY KINDS TO GROW. BOTH ARE BOG PLANTS.

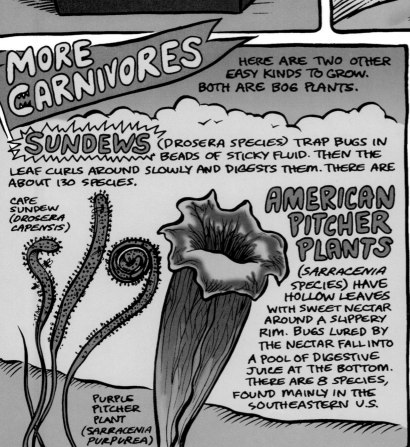

SUNDEWS
(DROSERA SPECIES) TRAP BUGS IN BEADS OF STICKY FLUID. THEN THE LEAF CURLS AROUND SLOWLY AND DIGESTS THEM. THERE ARE ABOUT 130 SPECIES.

CAPE SUNDEW (DROSERA CAPENSIS)

PURPLE PITCHER PLANT (SARRACENIA PURPUREA)

AMERICAN PITCHER PLANTS
(SARRACENIA SPECIES) HAVE HOLLOW LEAVES WITH SWEET NECTAR AROUND A SLIPPERY RIM. BUGS LURED BY THE NECTAR FALL INTO A POOL OF DIGESTIVE JUICE AT THE BOTTOM. THERE ARE 8 SPECIES, FOUND MAINLY IN THE SOUTHEASTERN U.S.

WEIRD BUT TRUE

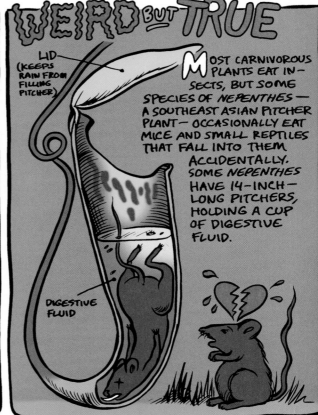

LID (KEEPS RAIN FROM FILLING PITCHER)

DIGESTIVE FLUID

MOST CARNIVOROUS PLANTS EAT INSECTS, BUT SOME SPECIES OF *NEPENTHES* — A SOUTHEAST ASIAN PITCHER PLANT — OCCASIONALLY EAT MICE AND SMALL REPTILES THAT FALL INTO THEM ACCIDENTALLY. SOME NEPENTHES HAVE 14-INCH-LONG PITCHERS, HOLDING A CUP OF DIGESTIVE FLUID.

TILLANDSIAS*

TILLANOSIA SPECIES

#Tih-LAND-zee-uhz

MOST PLANTS GROW IN THE GROUND. NOT *TILLANDSIAS!* THESE MEMBERS OF THE PINEAPPLE FAMILY INCLUDE MANY AIR PLANTS, OR EPIPHYTES (EP-uh-fights). THEY ABSORB MOISTURE FROM AIR, RAIN, OR POCKETS OF WATER WHERE THEY PERCH. MOSTLY, *TILLANDSIAS* PERCH ON TREES. BUT THEY ALSO SIT ON CACTI, ROCKS, AND EVEN TELEPHONE WIRES.

THERE ARE HUNDREDS OF *TILLANDSIAS*. MOST COME FROM WARM PARTS OF THE U.S. AND SOUTH AND CENTRAL AMERICA. MANY HAVE SPIKE-LIKE FLOWERS IN BRIGHT COLORS. TILLANDSIAS HAVE ONLY SMALL ROOTS, OR NONE AT ALL. THEIR LEAVES ARE WHAT GATHER WATER + FOOD.

TILLANDSIA RECURVATA, AT THE LEFT, GROWS IN THE MEXICAN DESERT. OTHER KINDS GROW IN HUMID SUB-TROPICS.

TILLANDSIA USNEOIDES—SPANISH MOSS—HANGS FROM TREE LIMBS IN THE SOUTHERN U.S.

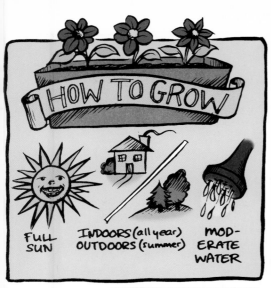

HOW TO GROW

FULL SUN

INDOORS (all year) OUTDOORS (summer)

MODERATE WATER

BUY YOUR TILLANDSIA AT A PLANT OR GIFT STORE. IT MAY COME GLUED TO A MAGNET OR A ROCK.

KA-put-meh-DOO-see

TILLANDSIA IONANTHA (ee-o-NAN-thuh) (LEFT), AND TILLANDSIA CAPUT-MEDUSAE (RIGHT) ARE WIDELY AVAILABLE. CAPUT-MEDUSAE MEANS "MEDUSA HEAD" IN LATIN.

KEEP YOUR TILLANDSIA IN A WARM, BRIGHT, AIRY PLACE.

SPRAY WITH WATER EVERY OTHER MORNING.

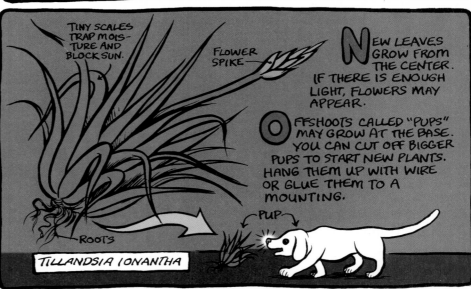

TINY SCALES TRAP MOISTURE AND BLOCK SUN.

FLOWER SPIKE

ROOTS

TILLANDSIA IONANTHA

PUP

NEW LEAVES GROW FROM THE CENTER. IF THERE IS ENOUGH LIGHT, FLOWERS MAY APPEAR.

OFFSHOOTS CALLED "PUPS" MAY GROW AT THE BASE. YOU CAN CUT OFF BIGGER PUPS TO START NEW PLANTS. HANG THEM UP WITH WIRE OR GLUE THEM TO A MOUNTING.

ABOUT EPIPHYTES

MANY DIFFERENT PLANTS HAVE EVOLVED TO GROW WITHOUT SOIL — INCLUDING SOME ORCHIDS, FERNS, AND MOSSES. THEY GATHER WATER AND FOOD WITH SPECIAL STRUCTURES ON THEIR LEAVES OR WITH HANGING ROOTS. WHY? HIGH UP ON TREES OR CLIFFS, THEY CAN GET MORE LIGHT THAN ON THE FOREST FLOOR. THEY DON'T HARM THEIR HOST PLANTS EXCEPT TO BLOCK SOME SUN FROM THE LEAVES.

LIVING STONES

(LITHOPS SPECIES)

THE STONY DESERTS OF SOUTHERN AFRICA APPEAR TO BE BARREN OF PLANT LIFE. BUT PLANTS ARE THERE, HIDDEN AMONG THE ROCKS. IN FACT, SOME LOOK LIKE ROCKS. THEY'RE CALLED *LITHOPS*, OR LIVING STONES.

THEY ARE EASIEST TO SPOT IN THE SPRING WHEN THEY BLOOM.

THEIR ROCK DISGUISE HELPS HIDE THEM FROM HUNGRY ANIMALS. EVEN PLANT EXPERTS MAY HAVE TROUBLE FINDING THEM.

EACH PLANT IS ACTUALLY TWO LEAVES STUCK TOGETHER.

1.
2.

SEVERAL OTHER PLANTS FROM THIS REGION LOOK LIKE ROCKS. LIVING ROCK (*PLEIOSPILOS BOLUSII*) IS ONE.

HOW TO GROW

FULL SUN   INDOORS   LITTLE WATER

CACTUS mix   HORTICULTURAL SAND   LITHOPS SEEDS

GET SEEDS FROM A CATALOG. IN A SHALLOW CONTAINER WITH DRAIN HOLES, MIX 4 PARTS CACTUS MIX AND 1 PART HORTICULTURAL SAND. MOISTEN.

SPREAD ABOUT 10 SEEDS ON THE SOIL (CAREFUL—THEY'RE TINY!). DUST WITH SAND TO PARTLY COVER. PRESS THEM DOWN.

1.

2. SEAL IN PLASTIC IN BRIGHT PLACE UNTIL SEEDS SPROUT (1-2 WEEKS).

3. REMOVE PLASTIC AND MIST DAILY UNTIL PLANTS ARE 8-12 WEEKS OLD. THEN WATER EVERY 2-3 DAYS, EVENTUALLY ONLY EVERY 2-4 WEEKS. POUR OUT DRAINAGE WATER OR PLANTS WILL ROT.

GROWN PLANTS ARE JUST ½-2" TALL. YOU MAY GET SEVERAL KINDS.

YOU'RE ALMOST AS OLD AS I AM!

TIPS

JAN FEB MAR APR MAY JUN JUL AUG SEP OCT NOV DEC

DON'T WATER FROM OCTOBER THROUGH MARCH—THE DRY SEASON IN SOUTHERN AFRICA.

NEW LEAVES EMERGE FROM BETWEEN OLD LEAVES, WHICH SHRIVEL.

OLD LEAF

LIVING STONES CAN LIVE OVER 90 YEARS—MAYBE LONGER THAN YOU!

PLACE GROWN PLANTS AT LEAST 3/4 INCH APART, WITH THEIR TOPS BARELY STICKING UP. YOU CAN PUT IN REAL STONES TO DISGUISE THEM.

HOW TO GROW

FULL SUN

INDOORS/OUTDOORS (SUMMER)

LITTLE WATER

Fabulous FIVE NAILS

HARDWARE

OPEN

STRING ON SALE!

GERTIE'S GLAMOROUS GARDEN SUPPLIES

SPECIAL THIS WEEK! STRING OF BEADS

JOYERÍA

PERLAS $10,000

LOTS OF PLANT STORES SELL STRING OF BEADS, SO YOU DON'T NEED TO BOTHER WITH SEEDS.

COME ON! SHHH!!

OH, DARLING! I JUST LOVE THIS FASCINATING PLANT!

KEEP YOUR STRING OF BEADS IN A SUNNY, AIRY PLACE. WATER ONLY WHEN THE SOIL FEELS DRY.

ALTHEA, YOU'RE AS LOVELY AS EVER!

FRANK? IS IT REALLY YOU?!

LEAVE ROOM FOR THE BEADS TO HANG DOWN.

TO START NEW PLANTS FOR FRIENDS OR RELATIVES, CUT OFF STEMS NEAR ROOTLETS AND STICK THEM IN DAMP POTTING SOIL...

OTHER WEIRD SUCCULENTS...

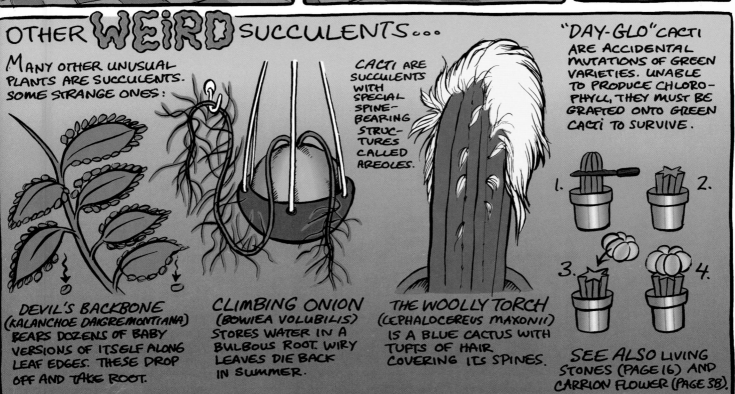

MANY OTHER UNUSUAL PLANTS ARE SUCCULENTS. SOME STRANGE ONES:

CACTI ARE SUCCULENTS WITH SPECIAL SPINE-BEARING STRUCTURES CALLED AREOLES.

"DAY-GLO" CACTI ARE ACCIDENTAL MUTATIONS OF GREEN VARIETIES. UNABLE TO PRODUCE CHLOROPHYLL, THEY MUST BE GRAFTED ONTO GREEN CACTI TO SURVIVE.

1. 2. 3. 4.

DEVIL'S BACKBONE (KALANCHOE DAIGREMONTIANA) BEARS DOZENS OF BABY VERSIONS OF ITSELF ALONG LEAF EDGES. THESE DROP OFF AND TAKE ROOT.

CLIMBING ONION (BOWIEA VOLUBILIS) STORES WATER IN A BULBOUS ROOT. WIRY LEAVES DIE BACK IN SUMMER.

THE WOOLLY TORCH (CEPHALOCEREUS MAXONII) IS A BLUE CACTUS WITH TUFTS OF HAIR COVERING ITS SPINES.

SEE ALSO LIVING STONES (PAGE 16) AND CARRION FLOWER (PAGE 38).

EASTER EGGPLANT

(SOLANUM MELONGENA VARIETY)

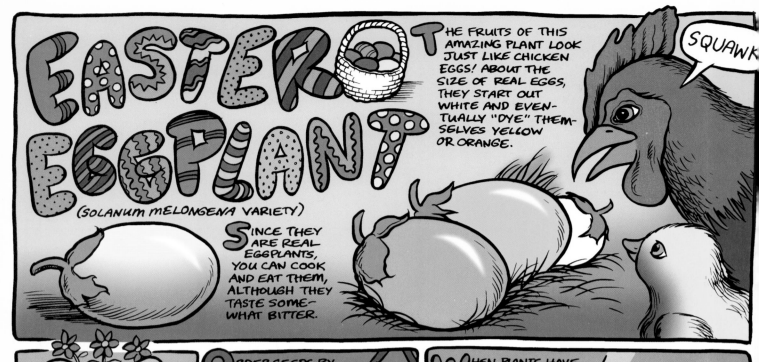

THE FRUITS OF THIS AMAZING PLANT LOOK JUST LIKE CHICKEN EGGS! ABOUT THE SIZE OF REAL EGGS, THEY START OUT WHITE AND EVENTUALLY "DYE" THEMSELVES YELLOW OR ORANGE.

SQUAWK!

SINCE THEY ARE REAL EGGPLANTS, YOU CAN COOK AND EAT THEM, ALTHOUGH THEY TASTE SOMEWHAT BITTER.

HOW TO GROW

FULL SUN

INDOORS +OUTDOORS

MODERATE WATER

ORDER SEEDS BY MAIL AND START THEM INDOORS IN LATE WINTER. PLACE THEM ON TOP OF POTTING SOIL IN A WARM, BRIGHT PLACE. KEEP THEM MOIST UNTIL THEY SPROUT.

WHEN PLANTS HAVE FOUR LEAVES, MOVE THEM TO BIGGER POTS NEAR A SUNNY WINDOW.

STIGMA
ANTHER

AS FLOWERS APPEAR, GENTLY BRUSH YELLOW POLLEN FROM THE ANTHERS ONTO THE STIGMAS TO ENSURE FRUITING. (OUTDOORS, WIND, AND BUGS NORMALLY DO THIS.)

OR YOU CAN TRANSPLANT THEM OUTDOORS, 2-3 FEET APART, IN LATE SPRING. "EGGS" DEVELOP WHEN PLANTS ARE 3-4 MONTHS OLD. UP TO A DOZEN MAY GROW ON EACH 1- TO 2-FOOT PLANT.

WEIRD BUT TRUE!!

EGGPLANTS, ALONG WITH TOMATOES AND POTATOES, ARE MEMBERS OF THE NIGHTSHADE FAMILY. BECAUSE THIS FAMILY INCLUDES SOME HIGHLY POISONOUS PLANTS—INCLUDING BELLADONNA AND HENBANE—THESE FRUITS AND VEGETABLES WERE LONG ASSUMED TO BE POISONOUS TOO. IN ENGLAND, EGGPLANTS WERE ONCE CALLED "MAD APPLES" BECAUSE PEOPLE THOUGHT THAT EATING THEM MADE YOU INSANE.

BOW WOW!

CHAPTER 2

Weird and USEFUL

THE WORLD IS FILLED WITH USEFUL PLANTS, INCLUDING SOME THAT ARE RATHER BIZARRE. THIS CHAPTER DESCRIBES SOME ODD ONES AND THE THINGS YOU CAN MAKE FROM THEM.

QUIZ

EVEN IN THIS AGE OF PLASTIC, MANY EVERYDAY THINGS ARE STILL MADE FROM PLANTS. CAN YOU MATCH THE ITEMS AT THE LEFT (←) WITH THE PLANTS THEY ARE MADE FROM (→)?

GASP

WELCOME

1. FIBER DOORMAT
2. PAPER
3. LINEN TABLECLOTH
4. BASKET
5. BATH TOWEL

A. BAMBOO
B. PINE TREE
C. COCONUT
D. COTTON
E. FLAX

ANSWERS: 1C, 2B, 3E, 4A, 5D.

WEIRD BUT TRUE

PEOPLE AROUND THE WORLD HAVE FOUND MANY INGENIOUS USES FOR PLANTS. A FEW EXAMPLES:

GOURDS CARVED WITH DESIGNS ARE MADE INTO BABY HATS IN NIGERIA.

PAPERY FLOWER HEADS OF THE "WEATHER GLASS" OR CARLINE THISTLE (CARLINA ACAULIS) ARE NAILED TO SWISS COTTAGE DOORS TO FORECAST RAIN. HUMIDITY IN THE AIR BEFORE A STORM MAKES THEM CLOSE UP.

CUPS AND DIPPERS MADE FROM BAMBOO SECTIONS ARE WIDELY USED IN ASIA.

WALKING-STICK CABBAGE

(BRASSICA OLERACEA LONGATA)

ENGLAND

The STEM CAN GROW 15 FEET TALL. AS IT GROWS, THE LOWER LEAVES FALL OFF AND LEAVE A KNOBBY WOODEN STALK.

The CHANNEL ISLANDS,

OFF THE COAST OF FRANCE, ARE FAMOUS FOR THEIR DAIRY COWS.

But A FAR STRANGER PRODUCT OF THESE ISLANDS IS THE WALKING-STICK CABBAGE. IT IS A REAL CABBAGE, BUT INSTEAD OF A COMPACT HEAD, IT GROWS LOOSE GREEN LEAVES ON A THICK CENTER STEM.

MOO.

ALDERNEY

People CUT DOWN THE STALKS AND MAKE WALKING STICKS OUT OF THEM. THEY FEED THE LEAVES TO FARM ANIMALS (THEY ARE TOO TOUGH FOR PEOPLE TO EAT).

GUERNSEY

SARK

JERSEY

FRANCE

HOW TO GROW

FULL SUN   OUTDOORS   MODERATE WATER

PLANT SEEDS IN A SUNNY PLACE IN SPRING. KEEP THE SOIL MOIST UNTIL THEY SPROUT.

WHEN THE SEEDLINGS COME UP, PULL OUT THE SMALLER, WEAKER ONES. THE REMAINING PLANTS SHOULD BE AT LEAST 2 FEET APART.

WATER ONCE A WEEK IF THERE IS NO RAIN.

PLANTS GROW 5-7 FEET TALL BY AUTUMN. IF YOU LIVE IN A MILD CLIMATE, YOU CAN KEEP THEM GROWING OVER THE WINTER, AND THEY MAY REACH 10-15 FEET.

HARVESTING + CURING

WHEN THE PLANTS ARE AS TALL AS YOU WANT, SAW THEM OFF CLOSE TO THE GROUND.

STAND THE STALKS IN A DRY, AIRY PLACE AND TURN THEM ONCE A MONTH. IN SIX MONTHS, THEY'LL BE READY.

TIMBERRR!

CREAK

SIGH!! MY SWEET LITTLE CABBAGE STALKS!

FINISHING TOUCHES

1. CUT THE STICK AS SHORT OR AS TALL AS YOU WANT IT.

2. SAND THE STICK WITH FINE SANDPAPER.

3. BRUSH ON SEVERAL COATS OF VARNISH OR POLYURETHANE (LET DRY BETWEEN COATS).

4. CAP OFF THE TOP AND BOTTOM WITH RUBBER CRUTCH TIPS.

PAPYRUS

CYPERUS PAPYRUS

In ancient times, this famous water plant grew all along the Nile.

Egyptians made many things from it: mats, sandals, ropes, small boats, and a kind of paper known as papyrus.

Scribes wrote and drew on papyrus sheets and scrolls.

As paper gradually replaced papyrus, the plants were no longer cultivated. But some are now being farmed again to make papyrus for tourists!!

Plants can grow 16 feet tall.

Umbels (flower heads) on top look like bunches of grass.

Stems are triangular and filled with spongy pith.

NILE RIVER

MOSES

The "bulrushes" in the Bible were papyrus.

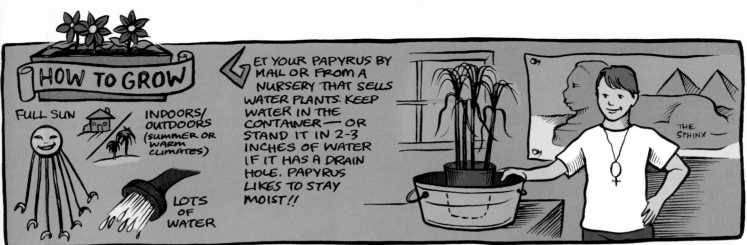

HOW TO GROW

FULL SUN

INDOORS/OUTDOORS (SUMMER OR WARM CLIMATES)

LOTS OF WATER

GET YOUR PAPYRUS BY MAIL OR FROM A NURSERY THAT SELLS WATER PLANTS. KEEP WATER IN THE CONTAINER — OR STAND IT IN 2-3 INCHES OF WATER IF IT HAS A DRAIN HOLE. PAPYRUS LIKES TO STAY MOIST!!

THE SPHINX

PLACE YOUR PAPYRUS BY A SUNNY WINDOW OR OUT-DOORS FOR THE SUMMER. IN FROST-FREE CLIMATES IT CAN STAY OUT ALL YEAR.

CUT OFF OLDER STEMS AS NEW STEMS GROW.

EACH SPRING, MOVE THE PLANT TO A LARGER POT FILLED PARTWAY WITH SOIL FROM OUTSIDE (DON'T USE POTTING SOIL — IT FLOATS!!).

MAKING PAPYRUS

HERE'S HOW YOU CAN MAKE PAPYRUS PAPER. THREE 3-FOOT STEMS WILL MAKE A PIECE ABOUT THE SIZE OF A BUSINESS CARD.

OTIS JONES

1. PITH. CUT INTO SHORT LENGTHS + SLICE OFF OUTER RINDS. SPLIT INNER PITH INTO FLAT STRIPS.

2. DO THIS 3 TIMES: SOAK 24 HOURS. ROLL OUT AND SOAK AGAIN.

3. LAY WET STRIPS SIDE BY SIDE ON A TOWEL.

LAY MORE STRIPS CROSSWISE. COVER WITH ANOTHER TOWEL.

PRESS UNTIL DRY (CHANGE TOWELS DAILY).

EGYPT ME!!
EGYPT YOU, TOO??
SECRETS OF THE MUMMIES
EGYPT TODAY
HIEROGLYPHICS MADE EASY

REMOVE PAPYRUS AND WRITE WITH ANY PEN!!

25

LUFFA GOURD
OR VEGETABLE SPONGE

(LUFFA AEGYPTIACA)

TENDRIL

LEAF

FLOWER

D RIED LUFFAS ARE USED AS SCRUBBERS OR MADE INTO SLIPPERS AND MATS.

Y OU MAY HAVE USED THESE SPONGELIKE SCRUBBERS IN THE BATH OR KITCHEN WITHOUT KNOWING THE REMARKABLE TRUTH ABOUT THEM: THEY ARE GOURDS. BUT INSTEAD OF FLESH INSIDE, THEY HAVE A NETWORK OF TOUGH FIBERS THAT REMAINS AFTER THE SKIN IS SOAKED AWAY.

T HE YOUNG ONES ARE TENDER ENOUGH TO COOK AND EAT LIKE SUMMER SQUASH.

DETAIL OF FIBERS

LUFFA FACTS

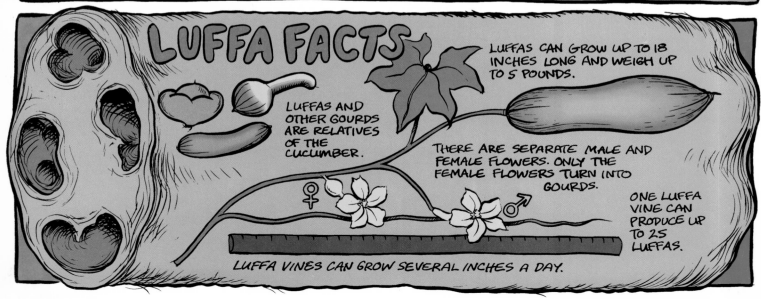

LUFFAS AND OTHER GOURDS ARE RELATIVES OF THE CUCUMBER.

LUFFAS CAN GROW UP TO 18 INCHES LONG AND WEIGH UP TO 5 POUNDS.

THERE ARE SEPARATE MALE AND FEMALE FLOWERS. ONLY THE FEMALE FLOWERS TURN INTO GOURDS.

ONE LUFFA VINE CAN PRODUCE UP TO 25 LUFFAS.

LUFFA VINES CAN GROW SEVERAL INCHES A DAY.

HOW TO GROW

FULL SUN   OUTDOORS   LOTS OF WATER

GET SEEDS FROM A STORE OR BY MAIL.

SOAK SEEDS OVERNIGHT IN A THERMOS BOTTLE OF WARM WATER.

PLANT ½ INCH DEEP IN SMALL CONTAINERS OF POTTING SOIL. KEEP THEM WARM AND MOIST. PLANT OUTSIDE WHEN THEY HAVE 4 LEAVES.

THIS VINE FROM TROPICAL ASIA NEEDS LOTS OF SUN AND WATER, AND SPACE TO CLIMB OR SPREAD OUT. SOME OF THE SMALL YELLOW FLOWERS WILL DEVELOP INTO 1- TO 2-FOOT-LONG GOURDS.

KEEP GROWING GOURDS OFF THE GROUND OR THEY'LL ROT.

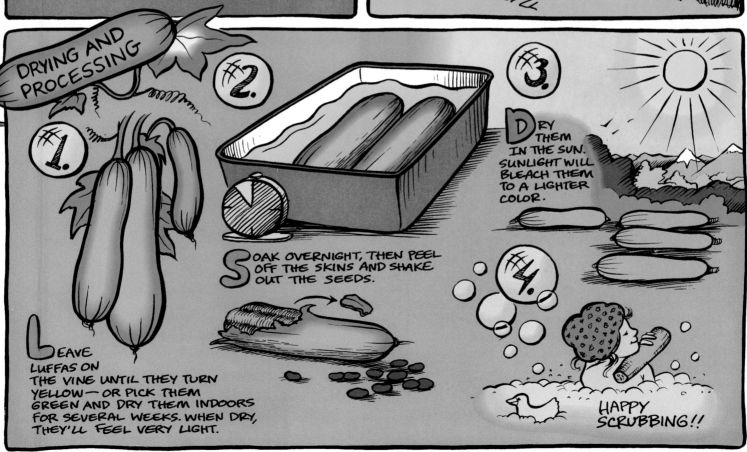

DRYING AND PROCESSING

#1. **L**EAVE LUFFAS ON THE VINE UNTIL THEY TURN YELLOW — OR PICK THEM GREEN AND DRY THEM INDOORS FOR SEVERAL WEEKS. WHEN DRY, THEY'LL FEEL VERY LIGHT.

#2. **S**OAK OVERNIGHT, THEN PEEL OFF THE SKINS AND SHAKE OUT THE SEEDS.

#3. **D**RY THEM IN THE SUN. SUNLIGHT WILL BLEACH THEM TO A LIGHTER COLOR.

#4. HAPPY SCRUBBING!!

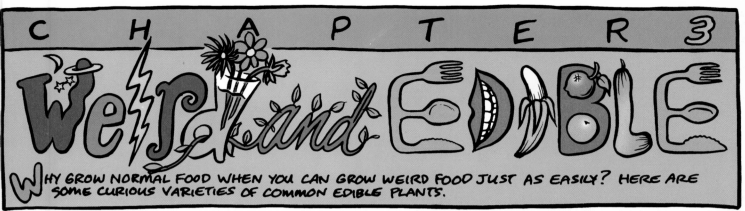

WeiRd and EDiBLE

WHY GROW NORMAL FOOD WHEN YOU CAN GROW WEIRD FOOD JUST AS EASILY? HERE ARE SOME CURIOUS VARIETIES OF COMMON EDIBLE PLANTS.

TRYING NEW FOODS

IMMIGRANTS HAVE BROUGHT MANY NEW FRUITS AND VEGETABLES TO THE U.S. HAVE YOU TRIED ANY OF THESE?

I PRESENT THE POTATO!

YUCK!

FROM **ASIA**:

STAR FRUIT

YARD-LONG BEAN

ASIA PEARL

GREAT WALL

FROM **LATIN AMERICA**:

PLANTAIN

TOMATILLO

SOMBRERO

MARIACHI

IT CAN TAKE A LONG TIME FOR NEW FOODS TO BE ACCEPTED. FOR EXAMPLE, POTATOES CAME TO EUROPE FROM SOUTH AMERICA IN THE 1500s, BUT IT TOOK YEARS OF ROYAL DECREES— AND FAMINES — BEFORE PEOPLE STOPPED BELIEVING THEY WERE POISONOUS.

WEiRD BUT TRUE ooooo.

MANY STRANGE BUT DELICIOUS FOOD PLANTS HAVE YET TO BE DISCOVERED OUTSIDE THEIR NATIVE LANDS. HERE ARE TWO FROM SOUTH AMERICA.

NUÑAS "POPPING BEANS"
PHASEOLUS VULGARIS VARIETIES

POD

UNPOPPED BEAN   POPPED BEAN

POPPING BEANS, OR NUÑAS (NOON-yas), ARE HARD-SHELLED BEANS THAT POP TO TWICE THEIR SIZE WHEN HEATED. THEY ARE EATEN AS SNACKS IN BOLIVIA, ECUADOR, AND PERU.

PACAY "ICE CREAM BEANS"
INGA SPECIES

ICE CREAM BEANS, OR PACAY (puh-KYE), ARE GIANT SEED PODS CONTAINING A SOFT, SWEET WHITE PULP THAT TASTES LIKE WARM ICE CREAM. THEY GROW ON TREES IN ECUADOR AND PERU.

POPCORN

ZEA MAYS VARIETIES

KERNELS of TRUTH

7,000 YEARS AGO   TODAY

ANCIENT CORNCOBS WERE LESS THAN AN INCH LONG. OVER MILLENNIA, FARMERS DEVELOPED LARGER COBS BY SELECTIVE BREEDING.

IN 1948, SCIENTISTS EXPLORING A PRE-HISTORIC CAVE IN NEW MEXICO FOUND 2,000-YEAR-OLD POPCORN THAT STILL POPPED!!!

EARLY CLAY POPCORN POPPERS IN PERU HAD CURVED SIDES TO KEEP CORN FROM FLYING OUT.

POPCORN IS A SPECIAL THICK-HULLED VARIETY OF CORN THAT POPS WHEN HEATED. FIRST GROWN THOUSANDS OF YEARS AGO IN CENTRAL AMERICA, IT WAS ONE OF THE EARLIEST KINDS OF CORN.

NATIVE AMERICANS POPPED CORN BY TOSSING IT ONTO HOT EMBERS OR STIR-RING IT IN CLAY POTS FULL OF HOT SAND. THEY TAUGHT THIS TRICK TO EUROPEAN SETTLERS.

WHY IT POPS

POPCORN KERNELS HAVE EXTRA-THICK HULLS THAT TRAP MOISTURE INSIDE. WHEN HEATED, THE MOISTURE EXPANDS INTO STEAM— AND THE KERNELS EXPLODE, TURNING INSIDE OUT.

POP!

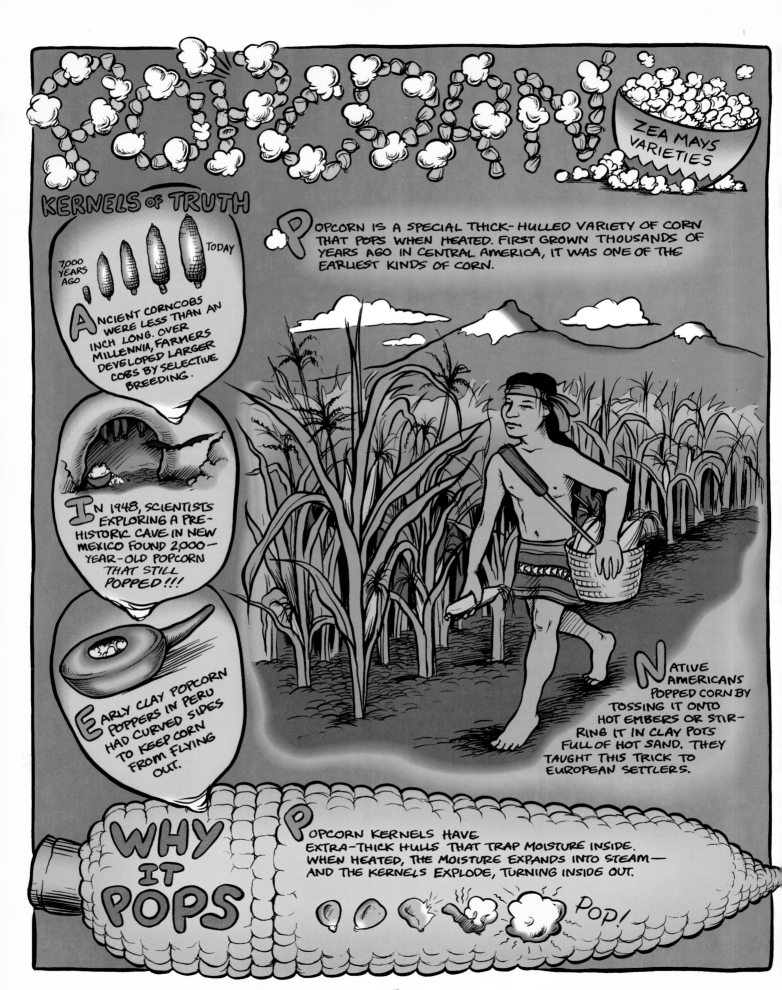

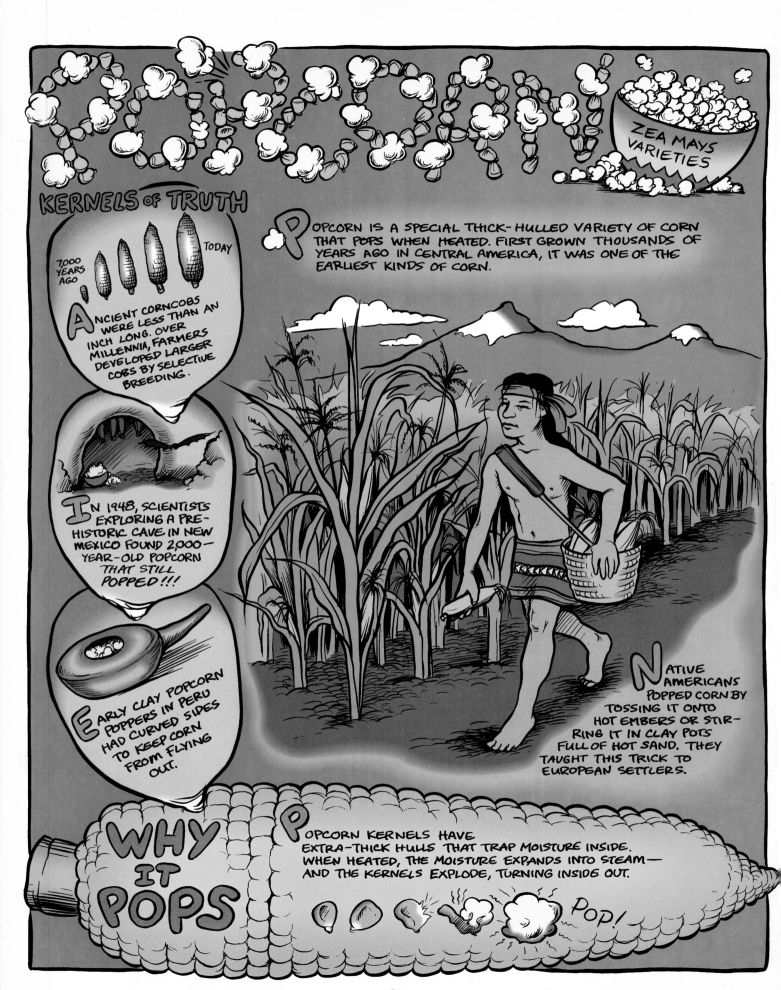

POPCORN

ZEA MAYS VARIETIES

KERNELS of TRUTH

7,000 YEARS AGO · TODAY

ANCIENT CORNCOBS WERE LESS THAN AN INCH LONG. OVER MILLENNIA, FARMERS DEVELOPED LARGER COBS BY SELECTIVE BREEDING.

IN 1948, SCIENTISTS EXPLORING A PRE-HISTORIC CAVE IN NEW MEXICO FOUND 2,000-YEAR-OLD POPCORN THAT STILL POPPED!!!

EARLY CLAY POPCORN POPPERS IN PERU HAD CURVED SIDES TO KEEP CORN FROM FLYING OUT.

POPCORN IS A SPECIAL THICK-HULLED VARIETY OF CORN THAT POPS WHEN HEATED. FIRST GROWN THOUSANDS OF YEARS AGO IN CENTRAL AMERICA, IT WAS ONE OF THE EARLIEST KINDS OF CORN.

NATIVE AMERICANS POPPED CORN BY TOSSING IT ONTO HOT EMBERS OR STIRRING IT IN CLAY POTS FULL OF HOT SAND. THEY TAUGHT THIS TRICK TO EUROPEAN SETTLERS.

WHY IT POPS

POPCORN KERNELS HAVE EXTRA-THICK HULLS THAT TRAP MOISTURE INSIDE. WHEN HEATED, THE MOISTURE EXPANDS INTO STEAM— AND THE KERNELS EXPLODE, TURNING INSIDE OUT.

Pop!

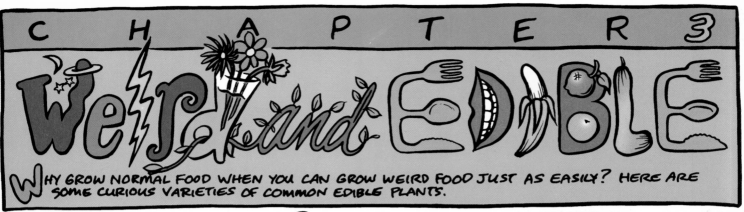

Weird and EDIBLE

WHY GROW NORMAL FOOD WHEN YOU CAN GROW WEIRD FOOD JUST AS EASILY? HERE ARE SOME CURIOUS VARIETIES OF COMMON EDIBLE PLANTS.

TRYING NEW FOODS

IMMIGRANTS HAVE BROUGHT MANY NEW FRUITS AND VEGETABLES TO THE U.S. HAVE YOU TRIED ANY OF THESE?

FROM ASIA:
- STAR FRUIT
- YARD-LONG BEAN
- ASIA PEARL

FROM LATIN AMERICA:
- PLANTAIN
- TOMATILLO
- GREAT WALL
- SOMBRERO
- MARIACHI

I PRESENT THE POTATO!

YUCK!

IT CAN TAKE A LONG TIME FOR NEW FOODS TO BE ACCEPTED. FOR EXAMPLE, POTATOES CAME TO EUROPE FROM SOUTH AMERICA IN THE 1500s, BUT IT TOOK YEARS OF ROYAL DECREES — AND FAMINES — BEFORE PEOPLE STOPPED BELIEVING THEY WERE POISONOUS.

WEIRD BUT TRUE....

MANY STRANGE BUT DELICIOUS FOOD PLANTS HAVE YET TO BE DISCOVERED OUTSIDE THEIR NATIVE LANDS. HERE ARE TWO FROM SOUTH AMERICA.

NUÑAS "POPPING BEANS"
PHASEOLUS VULGARIS VARIETIES

POD

UNPOPPED BEAN   POPPED BEAN

POPPING BEANS, OR NUÑAS (NOON-yas), ARE HARD-SHELLED BEANS THAT POP TO TWICE THEIR SIZE WHEN HEATED. THEY ARE EATEN AS SNACKS IN BOLIVIA, ECUADOR, AND PERU.

PACAY "ICE CREAM BEANS"
INGA SPECIES

ICE CREAM BEANS, OR PACAY (puh-KYE), ARE GIANT SEED PODS CONTAINING A SOFT, SWEET WHITE PULP THAT TASTES LIKE WARM ICE CREAM. THEY GROW ON TREES IN ECUADOR AND PERU.

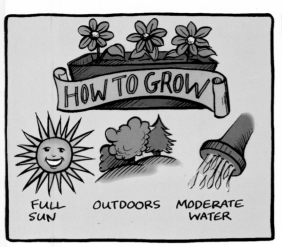

HOW TO GROW

FULL SUN   OUTDOORS   MODERATE WATER

GET POPCORN SEEDS (KERNELS) FROM A STORE OR CATALOG. INTERESTING KINDS ARE:

"STRAWBERRY" (TINY RED EARS)

"PRETTY POPS" (MULTICOLORED)

"MINIATURE COLORED"

ALL TYPES POP WHITE

IN SPRING, PLANT SEEDS 1-2 INCHES DEEP, ABOUT 1 FOOT APART, IN SEVERAL SHORT ROWS.

EACH PLANT MAY PRODUCE SEVERAL EARS. WIND BLOWS POLLEN FROM THE TASSELS (MALE FLOWERS) DOWN TO THE SILKS (FEMALE FLOWERS). A KERNEL FORMS IN THE HUSK AT THE BASE OF EACH POLLINATED SILK.

MALE FLOWERS

FEMALE FLOWERS

HARVESTING AND DRYING

LEAVE EARS ON THE STALKS UNTIL THE HUSKS ARE DRY AND BROWN. THEN TWIST AND SNAP THEM OFF.

PULL OFF HUSKS AND DRY THE EARS FOR 4-6 WEEKS IN A WARM, AIRY PLACE.

LEAVE KERNELS ON COBS OR RUB THEM OFF WITH A TWISTING MOTION. STORE COBS OR KERNELS IN AN AIRTIGHT JAR.

POPPING

YOU CAN POP WHOLE COBS IN THE MICROWAVE!

1. RUB AN EAR LIGHTLY WITH COOKING OIL AND PUT IT IN A COVERED GLASS MICROWAVE BOWL.

OIL

2. SET THE MICROWAVE TO HIGH FOR 4 MINUTES. WHEN 2-3 SECONDS PASS BETWEEN POPS— OR IF YOU SMELL BURNING— STOP THE OVEN EVEN IF THE 4 MINUTES AREN'T UP.

3. LET COOL BEFORE EATING!!

ROUND CARROT
DAUCUS CAROTA SATIVA

MOST CARROTS ARE LONG AND SKINNY, BUT A FEW VARIETIES ARE ACTUALLY ROUND. ABOUT THE SIZE OF GOLF BALLS, THEY CAN EASILY BE GROWN IN WINDOW BOXES AND FLOWERPOTS—INDOORS OR OUT!!

FULL SUN

INDOORS/OUTDOORS

MODERATE WATER

ORDER THE 'THUMBELINA,' 'KUNDULUS,' OR ANOTHER ROUND VARIETY FROM A SEED CATALOG.

IN SPRING, WORK SOME COMPOST OR HUMUS INTO DAMP SOIL AND SOW SEEDS THINLY, ½ INCH DEEP, IN ROWS 6-12 INCHES APART. KEEP THE SOIL FROM DRYING OUT UNTIL THEY SPROUT (8-10 DAYS).

OR START THEM INDOORS IN WARM, MOIST SOIL.

SNIP OFF WEAKER SEEDLINGS, LEAVING ONE PLANT EVERY 4-6 INCHES. THIS GIVES THE REMAINING CARROTS ROOM TO GROW.

TRUST ME!

OR INDOORS, MOVE PLANTS WITH 4 LEAVES INTO LARGER CONTAINERS WITH DRAIN HOLES. KEEP BY A WINDOW.

CARROTS ARE READY IN 10-12 WEEKS, DEPENDING ON THE VARIETY. OR YOU CAN PICK SOME SOONER + EAT THEM SMALL. THEY TASTE LIKE NORMAL CARROTS, ONLY ROUNDER.

THIS WHITE GIANT IS ONE OF SEVERAL EXTREMELY LARGE KINDS OF RADISHES FROM ASIA. KNOWN AS A *DAIKON* (JAPANESE FOR "GREAT ROOT"), OR *MOOLI* (FROM THE HINDI FOR "RADISH"), IT TYPICALLY GROWS 1½-2 FEET LONG AND 2-4 INCHES THICK. SOME VARIETIES GROW EVEN BIGGER. ALL TASTE SIMILAR TO WESTERN KINDS.

JAPANESE AND KOREAN COOKS SLICE THEM INTO THIN SHEETS TO MAKE EDIBLE FOOD DECORATIONS.

RAPHANUS SATIVUS VARIETIES

FULL SUN

OUTDOORS

MODERATE WATER

"COOKIE CUTTER" TOOLS FOR DAIKON RADISH

GIANT RADISH

GET DAIKON SEEDS BY MAIL. (SOME STORES MAY HAVE THEM). THE 'APRIL CROSS' HYBRID IS GOOD AND EASY TO FIND.

US MAIL

IN SPRING, DIG UP THE SOIL ABOUT 2 FEET AND MIX IN COMPOST OR HUMUS TO KEEP IT LOOSE. SOW SEEDS EVERY FEW INCHES, ½ INCH DEEP.

HUMUS

THIN SEEDLINGS SO THE REMAINING ONES ARE 16 INCHES APART. RADISHES ARE READY IN ABOUT 2 MONTHS.

16"

WEIRD BUT TRUE

THE WORLD'S LARGEST RADISHES COME FROM JAPAN. THE MORIGUCHI DAIKON GROWS UP TO 5 FEET LONG BUT BARELY AN INCH THICK. THE SAKURAJIMA DAIKON GROWS UP TO 2 FEET ACROSS AND CAN WEIGH UP TO 100 POUNDS.

MORIGUCHI DAIKON

WHEW!

INCH-WORM

SAKURAJIMA DAIKON

FLAVOR IMPERSONATORS

MINT THAT TASTES LIKE AN APPLE?!

THYME THAT TASTES LIKE A LEMON?!

GERANIUMS THAT TASTE LIKE PEPPERMINT OR SMELL LIKE ROSES?!

FLAVOR POLICE

YOU SAY IT TASTED LIKE A LEMON, SON?

YES, BUT IT SURE DIDN'T LOOK LIKE ONE!

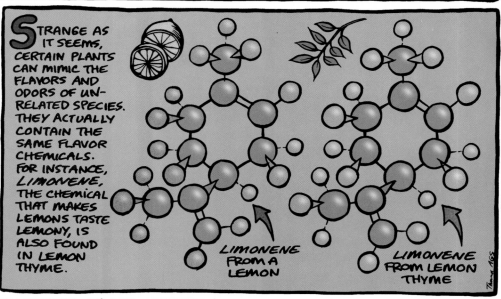

STRANGE AS IT SEEMS, CERTAIN PLANTS CAN MIMIC THE FLAVORS AND ODORS OF UNRELATED SPECIES. THEY ACTUALLY CONTAIN THE SAME FLAVOR CHEMICALS. FOR INSTANCE, LIMONENE, THE CHEMICAL THAT MAKES LEMONS TASTE LEMONY, IS ALSO FOUND IN LEMON THYME.

LIMONENE FROM A LEMON

LIMONENE FROM LEMON THYME

TO SAMPLE THE SCENT, RUB THE LEAVES BETWEEN YOUR FINGERS AND SMELL THEM.

SNIFF

OR YOU CAN SNIP OFF SOME LEAVES TO USE IN RECIPES.

EVIDENCE

There are many kinds of "flavor impersonators." Here are some that are often sold in garden stores or by mail. You can grow them in your yard or by a sunny window indoors. Buy plants rather than seeds, which may be hard to find.

APPLE MINT (Mentha Suaveolens, sometimes labeled Mentha Rotundifolia)

FLAVOR/SCENT: LIKE MINT + APPLES!!!

SOME SUN

INDOORS/OUTDOORS

MODERATE WATER

Mints come from Europe and Asia. They die back in cold winters but grow again in spring. Also look for pineapple mint (Mentha Suaveolens 'Variegata') and lemon mint or lemon balm (Melissa Officinalis).

LEMON-SCENTED THYME (Thymus x Citriodorus)

FLAVOR/SCENT: LIKE THYME + LEMONS!!!

SOME SUN

INDOORS/OUTDOORS

MODERATE WATER

Thymes are Mediterranean herbs that add flavor to meats or fish. Some kinds can survive cold winters. There's also a caraway thyme (Thymus Herba-Barona), which tastes like the seeds in rye bread.

SCENTED GERANIUMS

LEMON (Pelargonium Crispum)
PEPPERMINT (Pelargonium Tomentosum)
ROSE (Pelargonium Capitatum 'Attar of Rose' or Pelargonium Graveolens)

FLAVOR/SCENT: LIKE LEMONS, PEPPERMINT, OR ROSES!

SOME SUN

INDOORS/OUTDOORS (WARM CLIMATES)

LEMON GERANIUM   PEPPERMINT GERANIUM   ROSE GERANIUM

MODERATE WATER

From South Africa, scented geraniums can live for years indoors (or outdoors in warm climates). Flavor and scent are in the leaves, not the flowers. Other flavors include coconut and chocolate mint!

LEMON OR ROSE GERANIUM CAKE

1. Combine ingredients for a white cake (recipe or mix).

2. Spread washed leaves over wax paper at the bottom of a greased cake pan.

3. Pour batter over leaves and bake.

4. Add icing if desired.

Flowering Kale

BRASSICA HYBRIDS

FULL SUN   OUTDOORS   MODERATE WATER

Here is a vegetable so beautiful that it is grown as a flower. A relative of cabbage and broccoli, flowering kale has colorful, frilly leaves that grow in a radiating pattern like flower petals. It's the size of a large head of lettuce and tastes like a cross between broccoli and cabbage. You can cook the leaves or eat them in salads. Or you can just have fun admiring the plant.

Buy ready-grown plants in spring or fall... or...

Get seeds from a store or catalog.

Start seeds indoors in late winter and transplant them after frost ends. Or sow outside in spring or late summer. Flowering kale likes sunny garden soil with lots of compost or humus mixed in. It also grows well in flowerpots.

Keep the soil from drying out too much.

There are pink-centered and white-centered kinds...

Kale grows and tastes best in cool weather. If you want to eat any, pick it before the days get really hot.

You can harvest the whole head or just a few leaves at a time.

Weird and Beautiful

F LOWERS ARE AMONG THE MOST BEAUTIFUL THINGS ON EARTH—AND ALSO AMONG THE WEIRDEST, AS YOU'LL SEE IN THESE PAGES.

LOOKS ARE DECEIVING.

SWEET AND INNOCENT THOUGH THEY MAY LOOK, FLOWERS ARE ACTUALLY RATHER DEVIOUS. THEY USE TRICKS LIKE THIS TO SPREAD THEIR POLLEN SO THEY CAN MAKE SEEDS.

A S A BEE LANDS ON A PEA BLOSSOM, ITS WEIGHT TRIPS A SPRING DEVICE.

T HE FLOWER OPENS, DUSTING THE BEE WITH POLLEN AS IT REACHES FOR THE FLOWER'S SWEET NECTAR. THE POLLEN IS CARRIED TO OTHER FLOWERS.

O N THE RECEIVING FLOWER, EACH POLLEN GRAIN GROWS A TINY TUBE TO REACH AN EGGLIKE OVULE BELOW. OVULES RIPEN INTO SEEDS (PEAS).

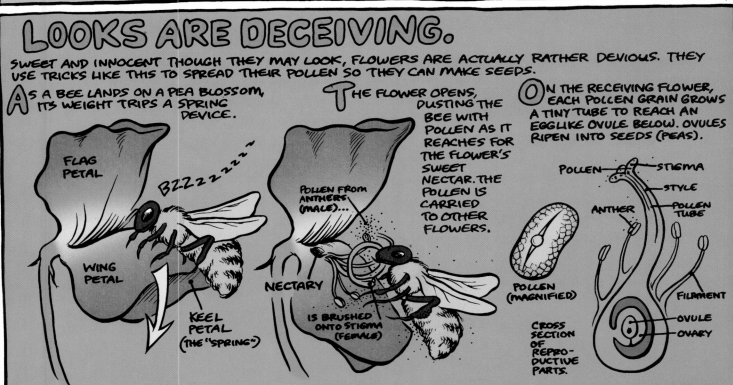

FLAG PETAL

BZZZZZZZ

WING PETAL

KEEL PETAL (THE "SPRING")

POLLEN FROM ANTHERS (MALE)...

NECTARY

IS BRUSHED ONTO STIGMA (FEMALE)

POLLEN (MAGNIFIED)

CROSS SECTION OF REPRODUCTIVE PARTS.

POLLEN — STIGMA
— STYLE
ANTHER — POLLEN TUBE
FILAMENT
OVULE
OVARY

WEIRD BUT TRUE

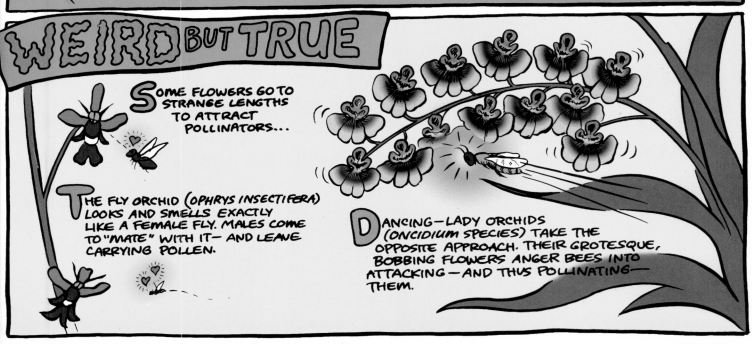

S OME FLOWERS GO TO STRANGE LENGTHS TO ATTRACT POLLINATORS...

T HE FLY ORCHID (OPHRYS INSECTIFERA) LOOKS AND SMELLS EXACTLY LIKE A FEMALE FLY. MALES COME TO "MATE" WITH IT—AND LEAVE CARRYING POLLEN.

D ANCING—LADY ORCHIDS (ONCIDIUM SPECIES) TAKE THE OPPOSITE APPROACH. THEIR GROTESQUE, BOBBING FLOWERS ANGER BEES INTO ATTACKING—AND THUS POLLINATING—THEM.

CARRION*FLOWER

(STAPELIA SPECIES)

YOU WOULD HAVE TO LOOK FAR AND WIDE TO FIND A PLANT AS STRANGE AS THIS. ITS CACTUSLIKE STEMS GROW LARGE, FLESHY FLOWERS COVERED WITH SPOTS OR STRIPES. SOME KINDS ARE HAIRY. ONE SPECIES, STAPELIA GIGANTEA, HAS 12-INCH-WIDE FLOWERS THAT ARE AMONG THE LARGEST IN THE WORLD.

BUT THE STRANGEST THING ABOUT CARRION FLOWERS IS HOW THEY SMELL—LIKE ROTTING MEAT!! IN THE WILD, THIS UNPLEASANT ODOR ATTRACTS FLIES, WHICH CARRY POLLEN FROM FLOWER TO FLOWER.

THERE ARE MORE THAN 75 SPECIES OF CARRION FLOWER.

yum yum

STAPELIA VARIEGATA

HYENA HYENA

CARRION FLOWERS ARE SUCCULENT PLANTS, WITH THICK STEMS THAT STORE WATER. MOST GROW IN THE DESERTS OF SOUTHERN AFRICA, NEAR ROCKS OR BUSHES.

* "CARRION" IS ANOTHER WORD FOR ROTTEN, SMELLY DEAD-ANIMAL FLESH.

38

HOW TO GROW

SOME SUN — INDOORS — MODERATE WATER

ORDER YOUR CARRION FLOWER FROM A NURSERY THAT SPECIALIZES IN HOUSEPLANTS.

DON'T BUY SEEDS—THEY TAKE TOO LONG TO GROW AND FLOWER.

HELLO!! THIS IS SAM THE BUTCHER!

DO YOU SELL CARRION FLOWERS?

HEY!! IS THIS A PRANK CALL?

WHEN THE PLANT ARRIVES, PLACE IT BY A BRIGHT (BUT NOT SUNNY) WINDOW. WATER IT WHEN THE SOIL FEELS DRY—ABOUT ONCE OR TWICE A WEEK. IN WINTER, WHEN THE PLANT IS RESTING, WATER EVEN LESS—BUT DON'T LET THE STEMS SHRIVEL.

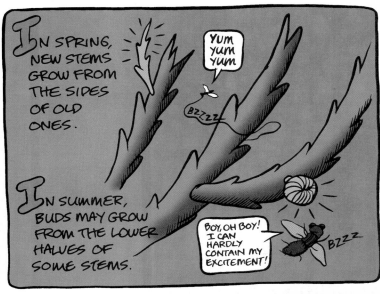

IN SPRING, NEW STEMS GROW FROM THE SIDES OF OLD ONES.

IN SUMMER, BUDS MAY GROW FROM THE LOWER HALVES OF SOME STEMS.

YUM YUM YUM

BZZZZ

BOY, OH BOY! I CAN HARDLY CONTAIN MY EXCITEMENT!

BZZZ

IF YOUR FLOWER GETS TOO SMELLY, MOVE IT OUTSIDE TEMPORARILY.

WEIRD BUT TRUE...

SEVERAL OTHER FLOWERS USE STINKING ODORS TO ATTRACT FLIES. THE STRANGEST ARE *RAFFLESIAS* (ra-FLEE-zee-uhz), FROM SOUTHEAST ASIA. THEIR REEKING, 3-FOOT-WIDE BLOOMS ARE THE LARGEST FLOWERS KNOWN. THESE PARASITES HAVE NO LEAVES TO MAKE FOOD WITH—THEY LIVE BY FEEDING OFF OTHER PLANTS' ROOTS.

BZZZZZ

BLACK FLOWERS??! GREEN FLOWERS?!

N OT MANY FLOWERS ARE BLACK OR GREEN, AND THERE'S A GOOD REASON: THESE COLORS DON'T ATTRACT BEES, BIRDS, OR OTHER POLLINATORS—AND ATTRACTING POLLINATORS IS WHAT FLOWERS ARE ALL ABOUT!

B UT BLACK AND GREEN FLOWERS STILL DO GET POLLINATED — BY THE WIND OR BY CHANCE VISITORS... OR BECAUSE THEY'RE NOT TRULY BLACK OR GREEN.

M ANY "BLACK" FLOWERS ARE ACTUALLY DARK SHADES OF PURPLE, RED, OR MAROON. PLANT BREEDERS HAVE CROSSED UNUSUALLY DARK PARENT PLANTS TO CREATE EVEN DARKER OFFSPRING.

S OME GREEN "FLOWERS" ARE REALLY ENLARGED CALYXES OR BRACTS—MODIFIED LEAVES THAT SUPPORT TINY TRUE FLOWERS OF A DIFFERENT COLOR. IN OTHER FLOWERS, THE PETALS ARE COLORED GREEN BY CHLOROPHYLL—THE SAME PIGMENT THAT COLORS LEAVES.

BELLS OF IRELAND
CALYX
TRUE FLOWER

BLACK + GREEN FLOWERS TO GROW:

SEE THE SEED OR BULB PACK FOR DETAILED INSTRUCTIONS!!

CARNATION

DIANTHUS CARYOPHYLLUS 'KING OF THE BLACKS'

START SEEDS IN A COOL PLACE. DON'T OVER-WATER PLANTS. WILL LIVE 1 SUMMER (LONGER IN WARMER CLIMATES).

HOLLYHOCK

ALCEA ROSEA 'NIGRA'

SET OUT AFTER LAST FROST. FLOWERS BLOOM ON 5-FOOT STEMS. MAY LIVE 2+ YEARS.

PANSY

VIOLA X WITTROCKIANA 'T+M'S BLACK PANSY' OR 'BOWLES BLACK'

START SEEDS IN A COOL PLACE. KEEP PLANTS MOIST AND SHADED. DIES IN FALL.

TULIP

TULIPA 'BLACK BEAUTY' OR 'QUEEN OF THE NIGHT.'

PLANT BULBS OUTSIDE IN FALL (6-8 INCHES DEEP, POINTED END UP). BLOOMS SEVERAL YEARS WHERE WINTERS FREEZE.

TASSEL FLOWER

AMARANTHUS CAUDATUS 'GREEN THUMB' OR 'VIRIDIS'

FLOWERS ARE SPIKES OR ROPES. LIKES WARMTH. DIES IN FALL.

BELLS OF IRELAND

MOLUCCELLA LAEVIS

THE GREEN "FLOWERS" ARE REALLY MODIFIED LEAVES. CHILL SEEDS AND PLANT IN LOOSE SOIL OUTDOORS, OR BUY GROWING PLANTS. DIES IN FALL.

NICOTIANA

NICOTIANA LANGSDORFFI

STRANGE HANGING "BELLS." PLANT SEEDS ON TOP OF SOIL- THEY NEED LIGHT. MAY LIVE SEVERAL YEARS IN WARM CLIMATES.

ZINNIA

ZINNIA ELEGANS 'ENVY DOUBLE'

WHEN WATERING, KEEP LEAVES DRY TO PREVENT MILDEW. DIES IN FALL.

Favorite Flower Colors

BEE

MOTH AND BEETLE

BUTTERFLY

HUMMINGBIRD

JUST AS YOU HAVE FAVORITE COLORS, DIFFERENT KINDS OF POLLINATORS DO TOO.

HOW TO GROW

FULL SUN

OUTDOORS

LOTS OF WATER!!

Get your water hyacinth from a store that sells water plants — or order it by mail. Because it has become a weed in warm climates, certain states may not allow it. The mail-order nursery can tell you.

When the days are warm, float your plant in a water-filled washtub, crock, or bucket. Keep it in the sun.

It will soon divide into more plants. If they get too crowded, cut off extras and throw them in the compost or trash (never in a lake or stream). Or give them to friends.

In climates with freezing winters, plants will die in the fall.

IT SURE IS GETTING CROWDED IN HERE!!

WEIRD BUT TRUE

Because their roots act like natural filters and they don't mind polluted water, water hyacinths are helping to recycle sewage. At a new kind of treatment plant near San Diego, California, filtered sewage flows into water hyacinth ponds, where bacteria digest it into small particles that plant roots can absorb.

This water — up to 1 million gallons a day — is disinfected and used to irrigate crops. If filtered some more, it could even be used for drinking!!

AQUACULTURE PLANT IN SOUTHERN CALIFORNIA

Everlasting Flowers

THE SAD FACT ABOUT MOST FLOWERS IS THAT THEY EVENTUALLY WILT, EVEN IF YOU PUT THEM IN WATER.

BUT SOME FLOWERS HAVE THE ABILITY TO STAY FRESH-LOOKING AND COLORFUL FOR MONTHS — EVEN YEARS.

CALLED "EVERLASTINGS," THESE REMARKABLE FLOWERS HAVE A PAPERY TEXTURE THAT SCARCELY CHANGES AFTER YOU PICK THEM.

HOW IS IT POSSIBLE? WE'VE BEEN AWAY ON VACATION FOR 2 WEEKS, AND HER FLOWERS ARE STILL BLOOMING!!

THERE ARE MANY KINDS — MOSTLY FROM DRY REGIONS, WHERE THE FLOWERS REMAIN COLORFUL DURING DROUGHT PERIODS.

44

HOW TO GROW

 FULL SUN

 **OUTDOORS**

 **MODERATE WATER**

THE FLOWERS BELOW ARE AMONG THE EASIEST AND MOST COLORFUL EVERLASTINGS. SEEDS ARE AVAILABLE FROM MANY STORES AND CATALOGS. IF YOU LIKE THESE, TRY AMMOBIUM, HELIPTERUM, AND XERANTHEMUM SPECIES ALSO.

GLOBE AMARANTH
(GOMPHRENA GLOBOSA VARIETIES)

NATIVES OF INDIA, THESE CLOVERLIKE, PAPERY FLOWERS THRIVE WHERE IT IS HOT AND DRY.

IN LATE WINTER, SOW SEEDS INDOORS ON TOP OF MOIST POTTING SOIL AND PLANT OUTSIDE AFTER FROST ENDS. OR START AND GROW IN A LARGE, SHALLOW FLOWER-POT.

PICK FLOWERS WHEN FULLY OPEN. PULL OFF LEAVES BEFORE DRYING.

STATICE
(LIMONIUM SPECIES & VARIETIES)

THESE MEDITERRANEAN "FLOWERS" CONSIST OF A DRY OUTER CALYX SUR-ROUNDING A SMALL FLOWER OF A DIFFERENT COLOR.

IN LATE WINTER, SOW SEEDS INDOORS 1/4 INCH DEEP IN MOIST SOIL. KEEP DARK UNTIL THEY SPROUT (1-3 WEEKS). PLANT OUTDOORS AFTER FROST (YOU CAN ALSO BUY SEEDLINGS).

PICK WHEN FLOWERS ARE THREE-QUARTERS OPEN.

STRAWFLOWER
(HELICHRYSUM BRACTEATUM VARIETIES)

THE COLORFUL PARTS OF THIS AUSTRALIAN FLOWER ARE THE PAPERY, LEAFLIKE BRACTS AROUND THE FLOWER HEADS.

IN LATE WINTER, SPREAD SEEDS OVER MOIST POTTING SOIL INDOORS. TRANSPLANT OUTSIDE WHEN FROST ENDS.

PICK WHEN THE FLOWERS ARE OPEN AND THE LEAVES HAVE DRIED OUT. REMOVE LEAVES BEFORE DRYING.

DRYING

ALTHOUGH THE FLOWERS WILL BE FAIRLY DRY WHEN YOU PICK THEM, YOU'LL NEED TO LET THE STEMS DRY OUT TOO. BROKEN OR SHORT STEMS CAN BE REPLACED WITH FLORIST'S WIRE.

TIE FLOWERS IN BUNCHES.

HANG THEM UPSIDE DOWN IN A DRY, AIRY PLACE. HANGING KEEPS THE STEMS STRAIGHT.

STEMS SHOULD BE STIFF WHEN DRY.

PASSION-FLOWER

PASSIFLORA SPECIES AND VARIETIES

THESE FLOWERS LOOK SO BIZARRE THAT YOU'D ALMOST THINK THEY CAME FROM SPACE. ACTUALLY, MOST COME FROM THE SOUTH AMERICAN RAIN FOREST— AND A FEW ARE NATIVE TO THE U.S. THERE ARE MORE THAN 400 KINDS.

EXOTIC AS THEY LOOK, PASSIONFLOWERS ARE EASY TO GROW AND CAN LIVE FOR YEARS.

SHALL WE HAIL THEM, CAPTAIN?

SOME SUN

INDOORS/OUTDOORS

MODERATE WATER

GROWING OUTDOORS

GET PLANTS FROM A GARDEN STORE OR BY MAIL— SEEDS TAKE TOO LONG. TRY BLUE PASSIONFLOWER (PASSIFLORA CAERULEA) OR, FOR VERY COLD CLIMATES, MAYPOP (PASSIFLORA INCARNATA), A NORTH AMERICAN NATIVE.

BLUE PASSIONFLOWER

MAYPOP

TRANSPLANT IT NEAR A WALL OR FENCE WHERE IT CAN CLIMB. IT GROWS FAST!

IF YOUR SOIL IS STICKY CLAY, WORK IN SOME COMPOST OR HUMUS FIRST.

FLOWERS BLOOM IN SPRING AND LATE FALL.

PLANTS DIE BACK IN COLD WINTERS BUT GROW AGAIN IN SPRING.

GROWING INDOORS

GROW BLUE PASSIONFLOWER OR PASSION FRUIT (PASSIFLORA EDULIS) BY A SUNNY WINDOW. ADD FERTILIZER WHILE BLOOMING.

WHEN THE PLANT GROWS BIGGER, MOVE IT TO A LARGER POT. YOU CAN TRAIN IT TO A STAKE OR AROUND A WIRE HOOP.

FLOWER

TENDRIL

THE PASSIONFLOWER IS A VINE. TENDRILS HELP IT CLIMB ABOVE THE DARK FOREST FLOOR— SOMETIMES 150 FEET.

PASSIFLORA EDULIS IS ONE OF SEVERAL SPECIES WITH EDIBLE FRUIT— THE PASSION FRUIT FOUND IN DRINKS LIKE HAWAIIAN PUNCH.

FRUIT

LEAF

KEEP IN TOUCH!

BYE!

WHERE TO GET THEM

To order the plants or seeds in this book, look up the plant names in the index below. The numbers tell you where to get them—for example, carrion flower is available from source 6, Logee's Greenhouses.

Plant Finder Index

Black flower—Carnation (seeds): 14
Black flower—Hollyhock (seeds): 9, 14
Black flower—Pansy (seeds): 9, 12, 14
Black flower—Tulip (bulbs): 2, 9
Carrion flower (plants): 6
Easter eggplant (seeds): 7, 9
Everlasting flower—Globe amaranth (seeds): 5, 8, 9, 11, 14
Everlasting flower—Statice (seeds): 2, 9, 12, 14
Everlasting flower—Strawflower (seeds): 5, 8, 9, 11, 14
Flavor impersonator—Lemon mint (lemon balm) (plants): 1, 4, 5, 6, 7, 8, 11, 13
Flavor impersonator—Other mints (plants): 4, 5, 6, 8, 11, 13
Flavor impersonator—Scented geraniums (plants): 4, 6, 11, 13
Flavor impersonator—Thymes (plants): 1, 4, 5, 6, 7, 8, 11, 13
Flowering kale (seeds): 9, 14

Giant radish (seeds): 8, 9, 14
Green flower—Bells of Ireland (seeds): 2, 5, 9, 12, 14
Green flower—Nicotiana (seeds): 9, 14
Green flower—Tassel flower (seeds): 5, 8, 14
Green flower—Zinnia (seeds): 12, 14
Living stones (seeds): 9, 14
Luffa gourd (seeds): 2, 7, 8, 9, 11, 14
Papyrus (plants): 6, 15, 16
Passionflower (plants): 5, 6, 11
Popcorn (seeds): 5, 7, 8, 9
Round carrot (seeds): 2, 8, 9, 12, 14
Sensitive plant (seeds): 9, 12, 14
Soapwort (plants): 1, 13
Soapwort (seeds): 8, 11
String of beads (plants): 6
Tillandsias (plants): 10
Venus flytrap and other carnivores (plants): 3
Walking-stick cabbage (seeds): 8, 14
Water hyacinth (plants): 15, 16

Sources

1. Bluestone Perennials
7211 Middle Ridge Rd., Madison, OH 44057
800-852-5243   Catalog free

2. W. Atlee Burpee & Co.
300 Park Ave., Warminster, PA 18974
800-888-1447   Catalog free

3. California Carnivores
7020 Trenton-Healdsburg Rd.
Forestville, CA 95436
707-838-1630   Catalog $2

4. Carroll Gardens
444 East Main St., P.O. Box 310
Westminster, MD 21158
410-848-5422   Catalog $2

5. Goodwin Creek Gardens
P.O. Box 83, Williams, OR 97544
503-846-7357   Catalog $1

6. Logee's Greenhouses
141 North St., Danielson, CT 06239
203-774-8038   Catalog $3

7. Mellinger's Inc.
2310 W. South Range Rd., North Lima, OH 44452
800-321-7444   Catalog free

8. Nichols Garden Nursery
1190 N. Pacific Highway, Albany, OR 97321
503-928-9280   Catalog free

9. Park Seed
Cokesbury Rd., Greenwood, SC 29647
803-223-8555   Catalog free

10. Rainforest Flora
1927 West Rosecrans Ave., Gardena, CA 90249
310-515-5200   Catalog $1.50

11. Richters
357 Highway 47, Goodwood,
Ontario L0C 1A0 Canada
416-640-6677   Catalog $2

12. Stokes Seeds, Inc.
Box 548, Buffalo, NY 14240
716-695-6980   Catalog free

13. Sunnybrook Farms
9448 Mayfield Rd., P.O. Box 6
Chesterland, OH 44026
216-729-7232   Catalog $1

14. Thompson & Morgan
P.O. Box 1308, Jackson, NJ 08527
800-274-7333   Catalog free

15. William Tricker, Inc.
7125 Tanglewood Drive, Independence, OH 44131
216-524-3491   Catalog $3.50

16. Van Ness Water Gardens
2460 N. Euclid Ave., Upland, CA 91784
909-982-2425   Catalog $6

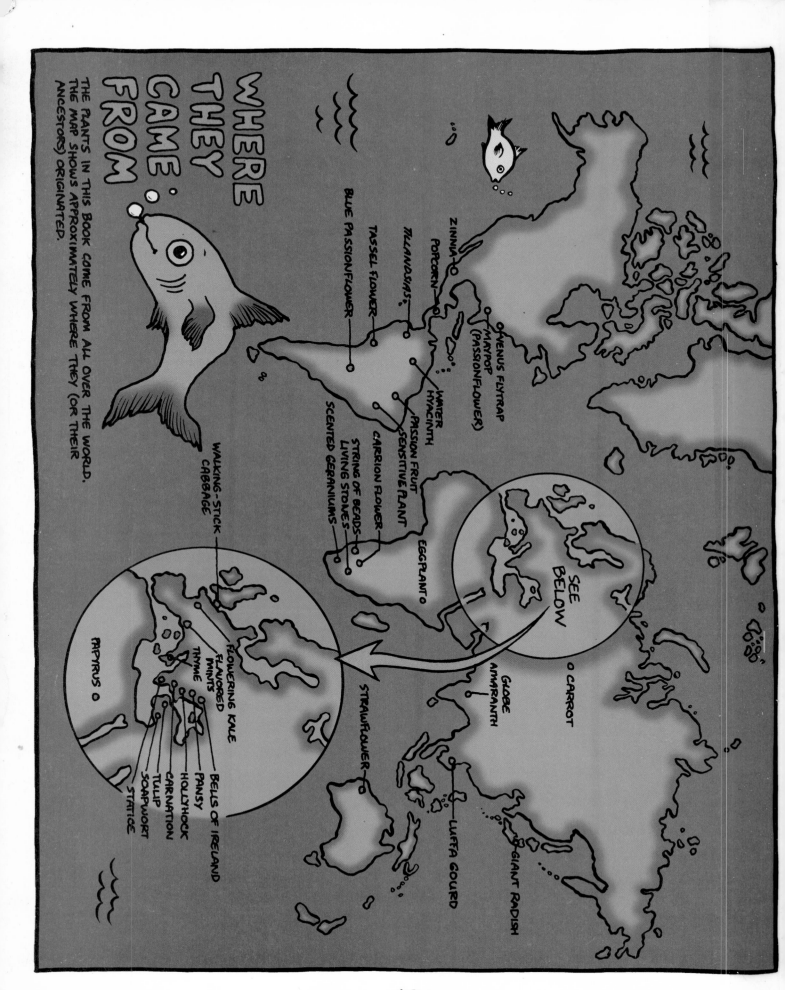

WHERE THEY CAME FROM

THE PLANTS IN THIS BOOK CAME FROM ALL OVER THE WORLD.
THE MAP SHOWS APPROXIMATELY WHERE THEY (OR THEIR
ANCESTORS) ORIGINATED.

ZINNIA
POPCORN
TILLANDSIAS
TASSEL FLOWER
BLUE PASSIONFLOWER

VENUS FLYTRAP
MAYPOP (PASSIONFLOWER)
WATER HYACINTH
PASSION FRUIT
SENSITIVE PLANT
CARRION FLOWER
STRING OF BEADS
LIVING STONES
SCENTED GERANIUMS

WALKING-STICK CABBAGE

EGGPLANT

SEE BELOW

GLOBE AMARANTH

CARROT

LUFFA GOURD

GIANT RADISH

STRAWFLOWER

PAPYRUS

FLOWERING KALE
FLAVORED MINTS
THYME
BELLS OF IRELAND
PANSY
HOLLYHOCK
CARNATION
TULIP
SOAPWORT
STATICE

48